# The Play About the Baby

*by*

**Edward Albee**

WITHDRAWN

**Methuen Drama**

Published by Methuen 2004

1 3 5 7 9 10 8 6 4 2

First published in the USA in 2003 by The Overlook Press,
Peter Mayer Publishers, Inc., New York

First published in the UK in 2004 by
Methuen Publishing Limited,
215 Vauxhall Bridge Road,
London SW1V 1EJ

Methuen Publishing Limited Reg. No. 3543167

A CIP catalogue record for this book is available from the British Library.

ISBN 0 413 77384 1

Typeset by SX Composing DTP, Rayleigh, Essex
Printed and bound in Great Britain by
Cox & Wyman Ltd, Reading, Berkshire

# The Play About the Baby

**Edward Albee** was born on 12 March, 1928, and began writing plays thirty years later. His plays include *The Zoo Story* (1958); *The American Dream* (1960); *Who's Afraid of Virginia Woolf* (1961–2, Tony Award); *Tiny Alice* (1964); *A Delicate Balance* (1966, Pulitzer Prize; 1996, Tony Award); *All Over* (1971); *Seascape* (1974, Pulitzer Prize); *The Lady From Dubuque* (1977–8); *The Man Who Had Three Arms* (1981); *Finding The Sun* (1982); *Marriage Play* (1986–7); *Three Tall Women* (1991, Pulitzer Prize); *Fragments* (1993); *The Play About The Baby* (1997); *The Goat Or, Who Is Sylvia?* (2000, 2002 Tony Award) and *Occupant* (2001). He is a member of the Dramatists Guild Council, and President of The Edward F. Albee Foundation. He was awarded the Gold Medal in Drama from the American Academy and Institute of Arts and Letters in 1980, and in 1996 received the Kennedy Center Honors and the National Medal of Arts.

*Also by Edward Albee*

The Zoo Story
The Death of Bessie Smith
The Sandbox
Fam and Yam
The American Dream
Who's Afraid of Virginia Woolf?
The Ballad of the Sad Café
Tiny Alice
Malcolm
A Delicate Balance
Everything in the Garden
Box and Quotations from Mao Tse-Tung
All Over
Seascape
Listening
Counting the Ways
The Lady from Dubuque
The Man Who Had Three Arms
Marriage Play
Finding the Sun
Three Tall Women
Fragments – A Concerto Grosso
The Goat, or Who is Sylvia?
Occupant

# The Play About the Baby

*The Play About the Baby* received its world premiere at the Almeida Theatre, London on 14 August 1998. The cast was as follows:

| | |
|---|---|
| **Girl** | Zöe Waites |
| **Boy** | Rupert Penry-Jones |
| **Man** | Alan Howard |
| **Woman** | Frances de la Tour |

*Directed by* Howard Davies
*Designed by* Tim Hatley
*Associate Costume Design by* Jackie Galloway
*Lighting by* Mark Henderson
*Sound by* John A. Leonard

*The Play About the Baby* was first produced in the United States in April 2000, in a production directed by Edward Albee, at the Alley Theatre, artistic director Gregory Boyd; managing director, Paul R. Tetreault.

*The Play About the Baby* premiered in New York at the Century Center for Performing Arts on 1 February 2001, produced by Elizabeth Ireland McCann, Daryl Roth, Terry Allen Kramer, Fifty-Second Street Productions, Robert Bartner and Stanley Kaufelt, in association with the Alley Theatre. The cast was as follows:

| | |
|---|---|
| **Girl** | Kathleen Early |
| **Boy** | David Burtka |
| **Man** | Brian Murray |
| **Woman** | Marian Seldes |

*Directed by* David Esbjornson
*Set design by* John Arnone
*Costume design by* Michael Krass
*Lighting design by* Kenneth Posner

# Act One

*Two chairs, identically placed not far from center, slightly diagonally towards one another, walking space between them. Nice light; neutral background.*

**Boy** and **Girl** *both seated,* **Girl** *hugely pregnant, she stage right, he stage left; hands folded, facing out.*

**Girl** (*not moving; calm*)    I'm going to have the baby now.

**Boy** and **Girl** *exit left.*

*Sound: growing labour; medical preps and encouragement. Growing pain and moaning; screams with accompanying sounds; slap; baby crying. Silence.*

**Boy** and **Girl**, *no longer pregnant, enter.*

**Girl** (*quietly*)    There.

**Boy** (*no comment*)    It's the miracle of life.

**Girl**    Yes; yes; it is.

**Boy** (*turns to her*)    Did it hurt a lot?

**Girl** (*touches her dress at the knee*)    They say you can't remember pain.

**Boy**    Aha.

**Girl** (*pause*)    Yes; yes, it did.

**Boy**    You *can*, then.

**Girl**    As I remember.

**Boy**    I broke my arm before I knew you. Did you know that?

**Girl**    Not that I remember.

**Boy**    Yes. Well, I did.

*Sound: cry of baby off-stage left.*

**Girl** (*rises*)   Feeding time.

**Boy**   In here.

**Girl**   All right. (*Exits left behind* **Boy**)

**Boy** (*sort of to her, but as if she is still there*)   It wasn't exactly I broke it; it was more they broke it for me. Not that they said we'll break it *for* you if you *want* us to – if you can't do it for yourself. (*Considers.*) More they just broke it – not *for* me, but rather as if I'd asked, though I hadn't. They did break it, though I hadn't asked. (*Afterthought.*) I'm sure if I'd asked they would have been . . . well, eager, I guess. That's only a supposition, though.

**Girl** *re-enters from left, already feeding the baby; she sits again, chair right. We do not see it, merely its blanket.*

**Girl**   Very hungry.

**Boy**   I'll want some; remember.

**Girl** (*slightly ironic*)   Line up!

**Boy** (*matter-of-fact*)   I'd come from the gym and I was pumped.

**Girl** (*looking down*)   V . . . e . . . r . . . y hungry.

**Boy**   The bloodrush, the endorphins . . .

**Girl** (*to* **Boy**)   I love your body; I really do.

**Boy** (*little wiggle of eyebrows*)   I know; I know you do. (*Back to previous tone.*) . . . And I was walking back to the dorm, and I had my gym bag and my stuff and I was . . .

**Girl**   When you let me lick your armpits I almost faint, I really do.

**Boy**   It tickles.

**Girl** (*smiles*)   You start getting hard.

**Boy**   Yes: it tickles. (*Previous tone.*) And I was in the alley between the gym and the science building and there were these guys I'd seen at the Hopeless Mothers gig at the arena when I was taking tickets there? And I'd spotted them trying to sneak in and I'd called the guards on them . . .

**Girl**  I like your left armpit better than the other.

**Boy**  Well, the other arm got broken; I was *telling* you.

**Girl**  You think that's . . . Ow! (*Reaction to baby at breast.*)

**Boy**  Let *me* at it for a while *I* won't bite!

**Girl** (*oddly*)  Not now.

**Boy**  I think I like both your breasts equally.

**Girl**  What happened?

**Boy**  Hm?

**Girl**  You called the guards on them – on the guys.

**Boy**  Oh, and the guards roughed them up a little, and they said, 'We'll get you, motherfucker!' The guys – not the guards. To me; they said it to me.

**Girl** (*looks at him*)  Yes: of course the guys, and of course to you.

**Boy**  And that's what they did.

**Girl**  What?

**Boy**  They got me, motherfucker. They said, in the alley there, hey, you're the one put the guard dogs on us, aren't you. I said yes, I was; guards, not guard dogs.

**Girl**  Not a wise answer.

**Boy**  Which?

**Girl**  Either; both

**Boy**  Never lie. Besides, they knew. Yes, I am, I said. You guys could have paid – benefit and all. You guys could have paid.

**Girl**  What was the benefit?

**Boy**   Mother's Milk.

**Girl**   Ah.

**Boy**   Yeah, I know, I know, they said – kind of apologetic; we shoulda paid. No hard feelings I said. Hey, no way, no way, they said. And I put my hand out: no hard feelings I said.

**Girl**   Less wise.

**Boy**   I know; and I think I knew what was going to happen, but too quick to stop it.

**Girl** (*looks at baby*)   Baby's full. (*Rises, goes off left, behind* **Boy**.)

**Boy** (*as she exits; as previously*)   I put my hand out, and I'd just come from the gym and my forearms looked great. (*Begins to demonstrate.*) And the big guy put his hand out and shook hands with me and swung around and cracked my arm against his knee and . . . Crack! And oh shit it hurt! Have fun taking tickets, the big one said, and the others laughed, and I was on my knees, and it hurt so much I was crying, and one of the others came up on me, and he unzipped his fly and what was he going to do . . . piss on me? I don't know; and the big one said leave him alone and they walked off. (*Pause.*) Maybe he *wasn't* going to piss on me; maybe he was going to . . .

**Girl** *re-enters from left.*

**Girl**   All asleep. (*Observes him on his knees, his disturbance.*)

**Boy** (*still preoccupied*)   I don't know what he was going to do! It hurt so! They hurt me so!

**Girl** (*she kneels in front of him, baring a breast*)   Shhhhhhh.

**Boy** (*softly; almost pleading*)   He hurt me so.

**Girl**   Come towards *me*.

**Boy** (*his left hand on her breast, his right arm hanging limp; still on his knees*)   . . . and the other one came towards me . . .

**Girl**   Here. Do this.

**Boy** (*his words becoming mumble as he fastens his mouth on her breast*)    . . . and he undid his fly, and I don't know what he was going to do. I don't know if he was going to . . .

**Girl**    Shhhhhh. Shhhhh. Shhhhh. Come. In here, in here.

**Girl** *leads* **Boy** *off left.* **Man** *enters, comes center and stands behind and between the chairs.*

**Man** (*out; smile*)    Hello there! (*Gestures off left.*) Boy, girl? Yes?

**Man** *observes chairs; passes fingers of right hand over stage right chair; smells fingers; considers; looks off left. Addresses audience; sighs.*

Ah . . . young smell! Have you ever noticed when you're driving somewhere you've not been before – directions, of course – it always takes longer than you think it should, that you've passed it, or not turned left when you were supposed to? And yet, when you're coming home, or whatever, *after* you've been there – the place you didn't know how to get to, but had directions – you're amazed at how much shorter the trip is? (*Fingers of left hand over stage left chair; smells fingers; eyebrows waggling; whispers.*) Young smell. Have you noticed that? Not young smell; how much shorter the trip is? I'm not sure whether it's it *does* take longer to get there, or it's it just seems so. (*To someone in particular.*) Have you noticed that? Hm? (*If no answer, go on; if there's an answer, improvise briefly.*) I don't think it's merely that it *seems* so, though it may seem that way – which may be the same thing but I don't think so: that which we *feel* we've experienced is the same as we have? (*Dismissive.*) Naaaaah! Reality determined by our experience of it? Or our *sense* of experiencing it? Naaaaaaah! (*Smells both hands together, then right, then left, then both again.*) Eeny-meeny-miney-moe! Have you ever noticed when you're talking to someone you should know, but don't, at a cocktail party, say, and you try to lead the conversation to remind you who they are – who you're talking to – they won't do it? They won't let you go there? Do they know what you're trying to do and are doing a kind of 'Fuck you. You don't remember me? Well, fuck you; just hang there!' Or are they so absorbed seeing you again, remembering *you* – perfectly, of course: your

name, the stuff you did to your wife – that it would never
occur to them you're twisting in the wind? Once, I was at a
party; well, no, I was *giving* it, and I was being a good host –
introducing people to people, putting types together I
thought would be good for one another or, sometimes, just a
hoot, or plain wrong – and I'd been at it for a while – it was
a big party – and I was groggy, I guess, and there was this
tall, older woman next to me – she'd sort of come over from
another group – and two dykes came up – middle-aged,
neither one diesel, neither one lipstick, real centered ladies –
and I'd known them for years, and they were Jo and Lu,
good simple, non-specific names: none of this Josephine and
Lucille shit – and I did my host act, and I turned to
introduce them to the older woman standing next to me, and
I looked at her, and I knew she was familiar, but I couldn't,
for the life of me, remember who she was, and I said, 'Jo, Lu,
this is . . . this is . . .' and Jo laughed and said, 'We *know* your
*mother*, dear.' (*To someone specific.*) Fall through the floor!! Ever
done that!? (*General again.*) I suppose that was the worst – so
far!, though I'm looking forward with a kind of dread –
fascinated dread, you know? After Jo and Lu had chuckled
off, Mother looked at me sort of funny and said, 'You
didn't know who I was, did you.' 'Oh, come on, Ma!' I said,
hearty guffaw. 'No, you didn't,' she said, just the fringiest
little bit sad, and she walked away. It didn't *change* anything
between us; we were okay, but I think it was the first time
I realized we were both adults. She died three years later.
(*To someone in particular; laughing.*) No! Not from that! (*General
again.*) *Nobody* dies from not being remembered. (*Change of
tone; more interior.*) From being forgotten, yes, very probably,
but not from being remembered. (*Pause.*) Or are they the
same *thing*? (*Thinks.*) No; not quite. (*Energy rising.*) So! Anyway!
I bring all this up because . . . well, clearly because I wanted
to bring it up, and I dare say there was a . . . Yes! Of course!
Driving somewhere you'd never been before, that was it; that
started it all. (*Smells fingers of both hands again.*) Ahhh! How
things fade – memories, photo-memories sometimes, last,
though, usually. *Scent.* (*Spells it.*) S . . . C . . . E . . . N . . . T

(*Sad now.*) All fades, all dissolves, and we are left with . . .
invention; *re*invention. I wonder how I'll remember (*gestures
about him*) all of *this*? But, since I'm not *there* yet – so to speak –
have not, haven't remembered it . . . (*brisk*) well, first we
*invent*, and then we *re*invent. As with the past so the future –
reality, as they laughingly call it? Who was it said 'Our
reality – or something – is determined by our need? The
greater need rules the game?' The reality? I guess that was
*me*. All those 'naaaahs' before? Remember the 'naaaahs'?
Just a trick. Pay attention to this, what's true and what isn't is
a tricky business, no? What's real and what isn't? Tricky. Do
you follow? Yes? No? Good. (*Shrugs.*) Whichever. (*Begins to
exit.*) Woman.

As **Man** *exits, stage left,* **Woman** *enters stage right, rather briskly;
sees* **Man** *exiting.*

**Woman** (*after exiting* **Man**)    Wait; wait! (*He exits.*) Am I
late? (*To audience now.*) Am I late!? Am I on time!?

**Boy** *enters, wearing a towel only;* **Woman** *sees him.*

**Woman** (*to* **Boy***; concerned*)    Am I late?

**Boy** (*mildly puzzled*)    Hello?

**Woman**    Hello. Am I late?

**Boy** (*matter-of-fact*)    I wouldn't know. (*Afterthought.*) Would I?

**Woman** (*fretful*)    I don't *know*!

**Boy** (*wipes his mouth; licks his lips; smiles*)    I've been mountain
climbing.

**Woman** (*overly bright*)    Have you!

**Boy**    Yes.

**Woman**    You hardly seem dressed for it.

**Boy** (*looks at his towel*)    Oh, I put this *on* . . . put it around
me.

**Woman** (*tiny pause as* **Boy** *doesn't continue*)   Oh? Aha! (*Pause.*) Where? Where did you put it on? I don't mean around your waist; I mean . . . where?

**Boy** (*points left, over his shoulder*)   In *there*.

**Woman**   No, I mean . . . (*Pause.*) Aha. (*Pause.*) Do you know who I am?

**Boy**   No.

**Woman**   Aha. (*Pause.*) Are you certain?

**Boy**   I'm not?

**Woman**   Aha. (*Silence.*) *Mountain* climbing?

**Boy** (*recalling; eyes closed, perhaps?*)   It's all jungle as you approach – well, as you imagine it: warm, warmer, moist; but you move through it, past all that, eventually, reluctantly, of course; you're coming up from the south – from below – and you see them up ahead, looming, but there is a lot to get through first, as I said, in the jungle there – the ridges, and the great declivity. God!, and it's so hot and moist and . . . and . . . thrilling, and . . .

**Woman**   I've never done it.

**Boy** (*looks at her oddly*)   Oh? (*Considers it.*) Well, quite probably not; not too many women do . . . what? Ten percent? I mean: I don't know you. (*Afterthought.*) Do I? (*Answers his own question.*) No; no, I don't think I do. So, no, you may not have – certainly not these; certainly not. (*Holds invisible melons toward her; on with his story.*) And . . . do you mind if I get hyperbolic here? Even *more* hyperbolic?

**Woman** (*cautious*)   I don't . . . *think* so.

**Boy**   Even more than I have been? I didn't think you would. And there are the deep ravines, and the ridges, and there are a lot of temptations! Well, one in particular – two! Two!! And you *do* stop there on your climb, on your ascent.

**Woman**   To rest.

**Boy**    Oh? (*Chuckles.*) No, not exactly; more to delve, I
guess; to explore; to absorb; to die a little. But you look up –
over the great sloping hill with all its jungle, and there they
are! (*Sighs.*) My goodness, there they are.

**Woman** (*helping*)    Snow-capped, jagged . . .

**Boy** (*slightly more disapproving*)    Who *are* you, lady!?

**Woman**    *Not* snowcapped? *Not* jagged?

**Boy** (*quiet*)    No; of course not: lovely, curving slopes, almost
twins. You go between them; there's moisture there; you
breathe; you press your ears gently between them and it's
the sound of giant seashells.

**Woman** (*gets it*)    Ohhhhhhh! Ohhhhhh, I see! *Those*
mountains; *that* climbing.

**Boy** (*puzzled*)    Yes, of course. What else?

**Woman** (*half to the **Boy**, half to herself*)    Hyperbole: of
course. (*Out.*) I should have known.

**Girl** *appears from left, naked, or as naked as the actress will allow.*

**Girl** (*to **Boy***)    What are you doing? Are you coming back
in? What are you doing?

**Boy** (*over his shoulder*)    Yes; right away.

**Girl** (*pointing to **Woman***)    Who is that?

**Boy** (*simply*)    I don't know.

**Girl** (*considers it*)    Oh. (*Considers it further.*) Well, leave her
there where you found her and come back in. You're not
finished; you're not there yet.

**Boy** (*backing left*)    Yes, I know. (*To **Woman** now.*) Yes;
goodbye; I'm not there yet.

*They exit –* **Boy** *and* **Girl** *– leaving* **Woman** *standing.*

**Woman** (*waves*)    Farewell, intrepid traveler. (*Waves off.*)
Farewell! (*Out.*) Where there's a boy, there's a girl, no?

(*Shrugs.*) Usually. (*Looks at the audience.*) Well. I . . . uh . . . well, I suppose you'd like to know who I am, or why I'm here. (*Some uncertainty.*) Well, I'm with *him*; (*gestures off left*) that's why I'm here; I'm with him. The man; not the boy. The man indicated me as he exited, said 'Woman' and exited. Remember? That's why I'm here – to be with him. To help . . . *him*; to . . . assist *him*. (*Hand up, palm out, to abort protest.*) I'm not an actress; I want you to know that right off, though why you'd think I *was*, I mean automatically think I *was*, I don't know, though I *am* a trifle . . . theatrical, I suppose, and no apologies *there*. I *was* Prince Charming in our all-girl school production of *Snow White*, and while the bug may have bitten, it never took. (*Chuckles.*) Nor – and forgive the seeming discontinuity here – nor am I from the press. That's the first thing I want you to know – well, the second, actually, the first being . . . having been . . . (*Trails off; starts again.*) Oh, I am a very good cook, among other things. I became that to please my husband, my *then* husband, who was in the habit of eating out, by which he meant . . . alone . . . without *me*. It occurred to *me* that if I . . . well, it was no good: alone, to him, meant *specifically* not with *me*, though with others, with lots of others. And the great feasts I'd prepare . . . would be for *me*. Alone. I became quite heavy, which I no longer am, and unmarried, which I am to this day. I trust he is still eating alone . . . all by himself . . . facing a wall. (*Pause.*) No matter. Really: from the very first week, come dinnertime, he would put the paper under his arm, say 'Bye-bye', or whatever, and . . . no matter. I *have* had journalistic dreams, though I am not a journalist – dreams of *being* a journalist, that is, and quite awake; not asleep. I went so far one time as to take a course; and my assignment was to interview a *writer*, to try to comprehend the 'creative mind' as they call it. (*Firm gesture.*) Don't try! Don't even give it a thought! There seems to be some sort of cabal going on on the part of these so-called creative people to keep the process a secret – a deep dark secret – from the rest of the world. What's the matter with these people? Do they think we're trying to steal their tricks? . . . would even *want* to!? And all I wanted to do was . . . under*stand*! And, let me tell you!, getting through to them – the creative types? – isn't easy. I mean even getting *at* them. I wrote politely to seven or eight of them, two poets, one biographer, a couple of short story writers, one female creator of 'theatre pieces,' etcetera, and not one of them answered. Silence; too busy 'creating,' I guess. (*On a roll now.*) I remember finally I bribed someone into giving me this one guy's agent's name – this novelist? – and persuaded the agent to call him and see if *I* could *call* him?, and maybe *talk* to him?, and finding out I could *do* that – with no guarantees, naturally – and calling, and hitting the brick wall of the novelist's male secretary. I don't *mean* anything by that, of course. (*Heavy wink.*) In any event, hitting *that* brick wall, having to repeat everything I'd said to the agent, and being told by the M.S. – the male secretary (*heavy wink*) – they'd get back to me, and waiting until finally they *did* – I mean, *really*, who did they think they were . . . *both* of them!? Finally, the M.S. *did* call me – I was in the touchy stages of a soufflé, naturally – telling me that *he* was there . . . (*Does fingers as quotes.*) 'Himself' that is: the famous novelist . . . and he *was* going to talk to me – 'himself' was – and I held the receiver to my ear, expecting what? – something other than a voice? I don't know – a choir of some sort? I held, and then his voice came . . . 'Here I am,' it said – *he* said – 'here I am.' Odd, no? And the voice wasn't friendly, or unfriendly, gruffer than I'd thought it would be, perhaps, just . . . noncommittal. 'Here I am; I'm here.' I almost hung up, but I didn't. I mean, I'd gotten this close, and if I hung up who *knows* when I'd get another . . . *you* know. 'I'm here,' he said. And I rushed through what I wanted. 'I'm studying the creative process, and I want to do it with *you*, through *you*, – watching *you*, understanding *you*.' 'You want to watch me while I *write*?!' he said, sort of incredulous, and I could sense the phone being passed back to the M.S., or just hung up, or tossed over his shoulder, or whatever. 'No! Wait!' I yelled. Silence. 'I'm waiting,' he finally said, no emotion at all. And I tried to explain what I really wanted.

**Girl**, *chased by* **Boy** – *naked, or close – go from stage left to stage right, a sweet chase, giggling, etc.* **Woman** *senses, sees them.*

What?! What was that?! Did two people just run nakedly across the stage, giggling? Yes? Well . . . why not? Where was I? Oh: 'What I really want is to watch you . . . uh . . . move your words from your mind to the page.' 'You're not serious,' he said, sort of . . . fading away. 'Oh, wait! Please; please!' I said – shouted, really. 'I *do* want to study you! I so want to watch you move your words from your mind to the page.' The sentence was beginning to sound strange to me. I heard a kind of chuckle from him . . . bitter, was it? Contemptuous? 'Well, that wouldn't be much fun for anybody but *you, would* it . . you underfoot, banging into people, asking a lot of ridiculous questions, studying everything, being an absolute . . .' 'I'd be a mouse! I'd be a mouse!' I said – (*shrugs*) mouse-like, I suppose. 'Yeah, sure!' he guffawed at me, right over the phone. 'Oh please; oh, please!' I whimpered. (*An aside.*) Have you ever noticed the way we say everything twice when we're upset? 'I'll be a mouse, I'll be a mouse;' 'Oh, please, oh, please!' Have you noticed that? *I* have. 'Will you? Will you? It'll only take a couple of weeks, and . . .' 'I'd rather die,' he said quietly . . . and he hung up. (*Indignation.*) What kind of people *are* they?! I mean . . . what kind of people *are* they, these . . . these . . .

**Girl** *and* **Boy** *repeat their previous stage cross, but from stage right to stage left.*

(*Noticing.*) Two people just ran nakedly across the stage again, did they not? Giggling? No? (*Businesslike.*) Well, then; now you know who I am *not*, what I do *not* do. As for who I am and what I *do* do, stayed tuned.

**Man** *enters.*

You've had me standing out here, vamping away . . .

**Man** (*amused*)   Shhhhhhhh; shhhhhhhh. It's fine; it's fine. Come along now.

**Woman**   What were you doing?

**Man**    Research? Peeing? Reparking? Whatever. (*Indicates off left.*) Boy and girl.

**Woman**    Yes; I noticed.

**Man**    That's them. 'That's they' doesn't sound right, though it is.

**Woman**    No, it doesn't. That is them, eh?

**Man**    Yes. How innocent they are.

**Woman**    Yes.

**Man**    Pure.

**Woman**    Yes.

**Man**    You'd think it was Eden, wouldn't you.

**Woman**    Yes. You would.

**Man**    Yes. (*Takes her hand; indicates out.*) Say bye-bye.

**Woman** (*out*)    Bye-bye

*They exit.* **Girl**, *followed by* **Boy**, *comes out, peers after* **Woman**.

**Girl**    Who *is* she? Who *is* that woman?

**Boy** (*looking after her*)    Very strange.

**Girl**    Yes.

**Boy**    I tried to talk to her. (*Correcting himself.*) *She* tried to talk to *me*.

**Girl**    And?

**Boy**    Very strange. She asked me if I knew who she was.

**Girl**    What did you tell her?

**Boy**    That I didn't.

**Girl**    Maybe she'll go away.

**Boy**    Maybe. (*Smiles.*) Can I chase you some more?

**Girl** (*giggles*)    No! No, you can't! It was fun!

**Boy**   Yes; yes it was. (*Decision.*) I'm going to chase you some more.

**Girl** (*delighted*)   You'll catch me. I'll let you catch me.

**Boy**   Will you let me roll you over, lay you down, and do it again?

**Girl** (*giggles*)   Maybe. (*Shyly sings*)
Roll me over,
In the clover
Roll me over
Lay me down

**Boy** (*joins in; they both sing*)   And do it again.

**Boy**   I like being on you.

**Girl** (*nice*)   I've noticed.

**Boy**   I like being *in* you (*Quickly.*) You've noticed; yes, I know.

**Girl**   Yes.

**Boy**   I like sleeping with you.

**Girl**   Yes.

**Boy** (*a smile*)   I like sleeping *in* you.

**Girl**   Yes.

**Boy**   Saves time.

**Girl**   Yes. Who *is* she? Who *is* that woman?

**Boy**   Is she familiar?

**Girl**   No, not exactly. I mean, she looks like a *woman*, but no; not at all; not familiar at all. (*An afterthought.*) A photograph, maybe?

**Boy** (*shrugs*)   She looks like a lot of people.

**Girl**   Yes. (*Abruptly.*) *Does* she?

**Boy**   *You* don't. *You* look like *you*.

**Girl** (*preoccupied*)    Oh? Does that make me happy?

**Boy**    It should.

**Girl**    Oh, well, then, it probably does.

**Boy** (*takes her wrist*)    Come with me.

**Girl** (*mild concern*)    Where?

**Boy**    In there. (*Indicates stage left.*) I want to *do* something.

**Girl** (*greater concern*)    What?!

**Boy**    Something new; something we've never done.

**Girl** (*slightly worried*)    There *isn't* anything.

**Boy** (*pulling her*)    I *read* about something. Don't fight me.

**Girl** (*some alarm*)    What *is* it?! What is it you want to do?

**Boy**    Relax into it. (*Lets her wrist go; hands to his chest, mock eloquence.*) You're my goal; you're my destination. You are my moon and sun and earth and sky and . . . (*breaks tone*) on and on, and so on and so forth. (*Grabs her wrist again.*) C'mon!

**Girl**    No! What! What *is* it?!

**Boy** (*an enthusiastic confidence*)    It hasn't been done for centuries; three religions outlawed it in the Middle Ages. C'mon!

**Girl** (*reluctantly giving in*)    W . . . e . . . l . . . l.

**Boy**    You'll *love* it. (*Mock tone again.*) You are my goal; you are my destination. (*Normal tone again.*) C'mon, girl, let's go!

**Girl** (*allowing herself to be dragged off*)    Not in front of the baby; whatever it is, not in front of the baby.

**Boy** (*slightly annoyed, as they exit*)    Okay; okay.

*After* **Boy** *and* **Girl** *exit,* **Man** *enters from right, playing blind.*

**Man** (*to the audience, but not looking at it, of course, and not facing it*)    The chairs should be right ahead of me . . . right . . . here! (*Wrong.*) No. Further? (*Bumps against stage right chair.*)

Ow! Yes; there it is. (*Opens eyes, turns to face audience.*) Did she give you a good time? Spin a splendid yarn? Yes? Good. She's good at that; she's very good at that. Have you ever done this? – pretended to be blind? I don't mean to offend those of you in the audience who *are* blind – physically blind, that is – though there are seldom many of you at plays – *blind*; deaf, yes; blind, seldom; which surprises me, since most good plays come at you 'by the ear,' so to speak; but, then again, so do a lot of bad ones – by the ear. The tactile is underdeveloped in the sighted – in the seeing – for the most part. I was at a museum in London a few years ago – at the Royal Academy, I *think* – and I came upon a sculpture exhibit set up especially for the blind. There were maybe twenty pieces in the exhibit – faces, abstract forms, a few animals – and there were guides about to help the blind get *to* the pieces; there were roped walkways, as well. The blind were asked to touch the sculptures, investigate them, while the guides would assist – the name of the artist, the materials, the subject if need be. I watched for a little, saw the wonder, the enthusiasm of the blind, their smiles, little cries, and then I decided to do it myself – be blind and go through the exhibit by touch only. I closed my eyes, and a guide came up to me, to help me. 'I'm not blind,' I said, 'except I'm pretending to be, to see it, so to speak, as a blind person would. Will you help me?' This being Britain – *or* me being lucky – she chirped at me: 'Of course! But be sure you keep your eyes tight shut!' And so I did, and it was fascinating – to see with my fingers, with my hands, to touch, as we sighted do in the dark, the way the blind do in their endless dark – in *their* light. There was a copy of that famous bronze sculpture of the wild boar in Florence, the one sitting on its haunches, front legs up? (*Demonstrates with his arms.*) The one with the bronze penis rubbed golden by the hundreds of years of Florentine men touching it – for good luck, for potency. (*Wonders.*) What about the women? Do *they* touch it? Have they touched it for centuries, at night, perhaps, in the dark? 'You're coming upon the Florentine boar,' she chirped – really, she *chirped*. 'Be sure

you touch its bits and pieces, for good luck.' 'It's w
said. 'It's . . . you know, its *thing*,' she said. 'Oh, right, I
I'd done it in Florence when I was there; but this was
different; this felt very different. (*Sudden shift; very offhand.*)
Have you seen the baby? Cute, no? They love it, *don't* they –
the baby. (*Some puzzlement.*) They really *love* it. I wonder how
much they love it? How much they need it? Perhaps we
should find out. As the lady said, stayed tuned. (*Puzzles more.*)
*Hunh*! (*A beat.*) Ah, well; off we go.

**Man** *exits*. **Girl** *enters, speaks off to* **Boy**.

**Girl**   That wasn't funny! Well, certainly not as funny as
you thought it was – was going to be.

**Boy** (*entering*)   Sorry. (*Not really.*)

**Girl**   It wasn't!

**Boy**   Sorry!

**Girl**   Mean it!

**Boy** (*genuine*)   Sorry.

**Girl** (*grudging*)   Well . . . maybe. I don't think I *like* being
thought of as a destination, by the way.

**Boy** (*nice*)   What would you *like* me to think of you as – if
not as a destination? I always *aim* for you: you *are* a
destination – *my* destination. I remember when I saw you for
the first time – when I was biking along – I saw you lying
there on the stretcher, all unconscious – I said – well, to
myself, more than to anyone – '*That's* the one; *that's* my
destination.'

**Girl** (*she's heard this before* )   That's sweet.

**Boy**   . . . And I said to myself, 'When she wakes up – if she
wakes up – I'm going to be there, and I'll be the first person
she sees, and she'll love me; she'll want me and she'll love
me; she's my destination.'

**Girl**   Yes; sweet. (*More interested.*) Did you *really* tell them at the hospital you were my brother? You told them you were my brother and that's why they let you in? Let you sit by me?

**Boy**   Yes. I wanted you very much and being your brother made it even more intense – made me hard.

**Girl** (*not too nice*)   So many things do.

**Boy** (*smiles*)   Yes. Isn't that nice?

**Girl** (*preoccupied*)   I wonder how that old Gypsy knew so much?

**Boy**   Who, the one you went to before we met?

**Girl**   Yes, the one who told me . . .

**Boy** (*sort of reciting*)   What, that you would pass out one day, be put on a stretcher and taken to the hospital, where nothing was found to be wrong – if fainting away is nothing – and that when this happened you would wake up and the nurse would be over you and she would smile and say everything was just fine and that your brother was in the hospital room with you, right by your side . . . that he was hard.

**Girl**   She didn't say that – either one, the nurse *or* the Gypsy – the hard part.

**Boy**   . . . And that when you looked and saw it wasn't your brother . . .

**Girl**   . . . not hard to determine, since I don't *have* one . . .

**Boy**   . . . it wasn't your brother, it would be the boy you would marry?

**Girl**   Yes. I wonder how that old Gypsy knew so much?

**Boy**   Was she really very old? *He* very old? Gypsies look older than they are.

**Girl** (*dogmatic*)    She was *old*. That's what the sign said: 'Come in and visit the old Gypsy; have your future told.'

**Boy**    They lie.

**Girl** (*slightly offended*)    No! It was all true! It all came true!

**Boy**    No: about being old. It might have been a man for all *you* know.

**Girl**    I can tell a man from a woman!

**Boy**    A Gypsy?

**Girl** (*uncertain*)    Well . . . (*More aggressive.*) What do you mean '*if* she wakes up'? What do you *mean* by that?

**Boy**    You could have had a stroke for all *I* knew; you could have been *dead*. But you were so beautiful – so thrilling – I assumed you weren't – wouldn't be. I got off my bike – didn't even look at it, left my clips on – and saw you there and my heart sang, as the song sings. She won't be dead, I said to myself; she'll wake up and I'll be hard and she'll love me and she'll marry me.

**Girl** (*preoccupied again*)    Gypsies are strange people. How *do* they know so much?

**Boy**    It's easy to foretell the future: you just have to know what's going to happen.

**Girl**    Hmmmmm.

**Boy**    And in the way of a true fairy tale come true no one even stole my bike.

**Girl**    I guess those boys weren't around.

**Boy**    What boys?

**Girl**    Oh, never mind.

**Boy**    Oh; those boys.

**Girl**    Never *mind*. What a lovely story.

**Boy**    *I* think so. Did the Gypsy say we'd have a baby?

**Girl**   No; the Gypsy was . . . well, she wouldn't *talk* about that.

**Boy**   Did you ask?

**Girl**   Of course! 'What about a baby?' I said. 'What about babies? How many will we have?'

**Boy**   And she wouldn't say – *he* wouldn't say?

**Girl**   No; she . . . the Gypsy frowned.

**Boy**   She *frowned*? He *frowned*?

**Girl**   'I can't see that,' she said; 'besides: your time is up.'

**Boy**   Your money, she meant – *he* meant: not your time, your money.

**Girl**   Same thing.

**Boy**   Yes. With Gypsies, yes.

**Girl**   Maybe we'd better go back, get some more answers; take the baby *with* us . . .

**Boy**   No! Gypsies steal babies!

**Girl** (*laughing*)   They don't!

**Boy**   You've never heard? It's famous; it's like the money scam.

**Girl**   What is *that*?

**Boy**   You don't know? The money scam? The Gypsy promises to double your money for you, so you bring it *to* her, or him, to be blessed, so it'll double, or whatever. You bring it in ten dollar bills, or something, in a big paper bag, and . . .

**Girl**   Why do you do *that*?

**Boy**   What?

**Girl**   Bring it to the Gypsy in a big paper bag!

**Boy**   To be blessed!

**Girl**    No! Why in a big paper bag?

**Boy** (*mildly irritated*)    Because that's the way the Gypsy *asks* for it.

**Girl**    Oh.

**Boy**    And the Gypsy puts the paper bag . . .

**Girl**    . . . with all the money in it . . .

**Boy**    . . . yes . . . *on* the table, *between* the two of you, and the Gypsy blesses it, and starts chanting, or something, and the music starts, and the lights go all funny . . .

**Girl** (*losing track*)    Wait a minute . . .

**Boy**    . . . and in the middle of all that the Gypsy pulls the famous switch.

**Girl**    *What* famous switch?!

**Boy**    Hm? Oh, the famous switch of the bag. In all the chanting and the lights and the music and all, the Gypsy switches bags – takes *your* paper bag with all the money in it and puts another paper bag in its place filled with – what, I don't know – newspapers, or something, cut-up newspapers.

**Girl** (*logical*)    Well, what if you opened it?! You'd see that . . .

**Boy**    . . . The Gypsy tells you to bury the paper bag in your backyard without opening it and without anyone seeing you, and you're to leave it there for – what? – three weeks, so the magic can work, the money can double, or whatever.

**Girl**    Yes, but . . .

**Boy**    . . . And you do it, because you're an asshole – you wouldn't have put your life savings in a paper bag and handed it to some damn Gypsy if you *weren't* an asshole in the first place. And so, after three weeks you go out and starting digging up your backyard, since you've probably forgotten exactly where you've buried the paper bag, you

being such an asshole, and your husband asks you what you're doing, and there's nothing for it, and so you say you're digging up the paper bag with all your life savings in it, like the Gypsy told you to do. And your *husband*, who knows a lot more about Gypsies than *you* do, is sitting down by now, his head in his hands, crying. And so you eventually find where you buried it, and you dig it up and you take it over to your husband to show him how the money's doubled, and you open up the bag . . .

**Girl**   . . . and it's all cut-up newspaper.

**Boy**   Right; and the Gypsy's probably in Miami Beach by now driving around in some snazzy convertible.

**Girl** (*at a loss for words*)   That's . . . that's . . . *terrible*.

**Boy**   You bet your life *savings* it is. So you don't take the baby to the Gypsies.

**Girl**   They'd steal it.

**Boy**   Probably.

**Girl**   But, what would they . . . *do* with it?

**Boy** (*shrugs*)   Sell it. Eat it.

**Girl** (*disbelieving*)   Noooooooo!

**Boy** (*shrugs again*)   Okay.

**Man** (*pops in*)   If you're not careful you're going to have the Society for the Prevention of Cruelty to Gypsies after you. (*Exits abruptly.*)

**Boy** (*to where he was; nonplussed*)   Why? Why would I?

**Girl**   Who *is* that *man*! Why are there so many strange people around here?

**Boy** (*at* **Girl***; preoccupied*)   What? What? (*To where* **Man** *was.*) Nobody cares about *Gypsies*! (*To* **Girl**.) *What* strange people?

**Girl**    You were talking to a woman earlier, and now this man sticks his head in here and . . .

**Boy** (*shrugs*)    *I* don't know these people. I thought we were talking about the baby.

**Girl**    We were; indeed we were. Do we have in-laws we don't know about?

**Boy**    Not that I know of.

**Girl**    Have we rented out rooms?

**Boy**    I don't believe so.

**Girl**    Then why are they here? (*Suddenly.*) Maybe they're Gypsies! Come to steal the baby!

**Boy**    Don't *you* be so silly. Do they *look* like Gypsies?

**Girl**    Well . . .

**Boy**    Swarthy; big mustaches, cigars, fedoras . . .

**Girl**    Like Mexicans?

**Boy**    No; different. Mexicans wear little derbies.

**Girl**    That's Peruvians, and that's women.

**Boy** (*mildly annoyed*)    Whatever. Mexicans look . . . Mexican. Gypsies – from photographs I've seen . . . drawings – look like . . . well, like Gypsies.

**Girl**    Oh. (*Relieved.*) Then they're not Gypsies come to steal the baby.

**Boy**    What I said was, these people don't *look* like Gypsies – from what I know of how Gypsies look – which may not be much. That's what I said. (*Pause.*) Why would anybody want to steal the baby?

**Girl**    For money?

**Boy**    We don't have any.

**Girl**    To sell it, or to eat it?

**Boy** (*sighing*)   I said that's what Gypsies are *purported* to do, and I said I didn't think that . . .

**Girl** (*abrupt*)   All *right*! (*Shy.*) To *hurt* us? To injure us beyond salvation?

**Boy** (*pause; very sincere*)   Aren't we too young?

**Girl** (*not wholly convinced*)   I suppose.

*Baby crying off-stage.*

**Girl** (*alarmed*)   The baby's crying! Do you think someone is . . .

**Boy** (*comforting*)   Doesn't that sound like hunger? Isn't that the hungry sound the baby makes?

**Girl** (*somewhat relieved*)   Yes; yes; I suppose so. (*Moves to exit.*) I'll go feed the baby. (*Exits.*)

**Man** (*half to himself; very preoccupied*)   Leave some for me. (*Pause.*)

*This next speech is to 'theoretical people.' The audience is not to be addressed directly, nor is anyone else.*

**Boy**   Beyond salvation? Injure us beyond salvation? Hurt us to the point that . . . ? (*To* **Girl**, *off.*) I'm standing guard. (*She doesn't hear, of course. More to himself now.*) I'll guard you; I'll guard the baby. (*Gentle.*) If there's anybody out there wants to do this to us – to hurt us so – ask *why*? Ask what we've *done*? I can take pain and loss and all the rest *later* – I *think* I can, when it comes as natural as . . . sleep? but . . . now? We're *happy*; we love each other; I'm hard all the time; we have a baby. We don't even under*stand* each other yet! (*Pause.*) So . . . give it some thought. Give us some time. (*Pause.*) Okay?

**Girl** (*emerges; goes to* **Boy**)   Wasn't hungry; false alarm.

**Boy** (*shrugs*)   No problem. (*Out again.*) Okay? Please?

**Man** *is propelled on-stage; followed by* **Woman***; clearly they are in the middle of a heated exchange.*

**Woman**   I was young once, remember? I had a life before you?

**Man**   Oh, God!

**Woman**   What you referred to – what you always refer to – as my privileged little life before I met you?

**Man**   Oh, God! (*Indicates out.*) Not in front of all these people! (*Indicates* **Boy** *and* **Girl** *who are peripheral.*) Not in front of the children!

*They stand, sit, move; musical chairs, etc.*

**Woman**   Well, I *did* have. You think no one but you wanted me? Hunh?! (*A pronouncement.*) A painter hanged himself for the love of me.

**Man** (*flat contradiction*)   No.

**Woman**   Yes, he *did*. I was eighteen, and moving into ripeness. I was eighteen, as I said, and knowledgeable, and I was at a tea one afternoon – it was summer; it was a resort – and I had on silk and a great hat with ribbons, and I had been to Europe . . .

**Man** (*quietly dogmatic*)   You had *not*. (*To* **Boy** *and* **Girl**.) She had not!

**Woman** (*overriding him*)   . . . and I had been to Europe, and I knew the women there went without bras if their breasts were exemplary and if they were young, and I had my lovely breasts. (*Cups them for him.*) Lovely? Breasts? (*Tiny pause.*) Nothing?

**Man**   Get on with it.

**Woman** (*smiles*)   And I had my lovely breasts free in the delicious silk, an unlined silk, smooth against my nipples; and I stalked about – I think I had a parasol as well, really doing it up. Very Gainsborough, or perhaps Watteau.

**Man**   Jesus!

**Woman**   'Very Gainsborough, or perhaps Watteau,' I
heard a voice say, just behind me and to the right. I
stopped. I mean, who else could the voice be referring to,
right?

**Man** (*ironic*)   Right!

**Woman**   'Definitely Watteau,' it went on, 'definitely
Watteau.' And I turned my pretty head, and there he was
. . . The Painter. Not a man who painted, not a painter, but
. . . The Painter: hollow-cheeked, burning eyes, wispy
whiskers, long, bony fingers, the voice cavernous, *basso*, the
costume . . . well, do you know Whistler? (*Afterthought.*) Of
course you do.

**Man**   Of course I do.

**Woman**   Of course you do.

**Man**   What do you take me for?

**Woman**   'You should have a crook and sheep, or an arm
basket filled with wild-flowers. I'm going to paint you,' he
said. '*Are* you!' I said.

**Man** (*out*)   I don't believe a word of this. (*To* **Boy** *and*
**Girl**.) Not a word of this is true.

**Woman**   'Yes,' he said, 'twice.' 'To get it right?' I joked.
'First time a practice swing?' 'No,' he said, his burning eyes
even deeper and sadder, 'first as you are, as you are right
now, and then, later, naked, your lovely breasts, the dimple
of your belly, your milk-pink hips, your burning bush . . .'
'Really!' I said, 'You go too far!' Phrases like that just . . .
came to me then; I could do them with conviction. 'Really,
sir, you go too far.'

**Man** (*back in*)   Milk-pink?

**Woman** (*a triple embarrassed*)   Well . . . yes.

**Man**   You must have read it somewhere. (*To* **Boy** *and*
**Girl**.) She read it somewhere.

**Woman** (*high horse*)   It is what he said! (*Back to recounting; out.*) I should probably interject here that all my lovers to that moment had been both young and handsome – sturdy, virile boys and young men my own age, well-muscled . . . handsome, as I said. I had not made love with the aged, with cripples, dwarves, or – and I blush at this, I think, in retrospect, at least, for its lack of humor, its lack of generosity – even with the simply plain.

**Man** (*eyes to heaven*)   Christ!

**Woman** (*back in*)   Needless to say – needles, as I used to say when I was little – *almost* needles to say nothing was further from my lovely mind than an affair with the gaunt and disheveled painter. (*Thinks.*) Well . . . perhaps death was further from my mind, but not much. I was seeing – as they say – 'seeing' a young polo player . . .

**Man** (*out*)   Do you believe *any* of this? (*To **Boy** and **Girl**.*) Do you? (*Afterthought.*) Well, *they* might.

**Woman**   Yes, of course they do . . . a young polo player, whose biceps alone were worth the trip. I was seeing him, and quite involved, almost . . . happy. What did I need with . . . well, with anything else? My days were filled with polo, my nights with rut. Oh, what a wangled teb we weave.

**Man**   A what

**Woman**   A teb; a wangled teb.

**Man**   What is *that*?

**Woman**   *You* figure it out. Anyway, I sat for the painter. He was meticulous, and he worked so slowly. My polo player wondered where I was instead of watching him knock balls through the legs of horses. 'I'm being painted as a shepherdess,' I said. 'You're kidding!' he replied, white teeth flashing, et cetera. 'Be careful he doesn't want to paint you in the nude,' he warned. 'Oh, he does,' I smiled, 'he does.' And Beauty's face darkened – even beneath the tan – and my young heart broke, for I saw that he loved me, and I knew in that moment . . . that I did not love him.

**Man**   Oh, you poor dear!

**Woman**   That I *desired* him, yes; I mean, he *was* a splendid lover – slow, patient, thoughtful, but always in command, and driving. Indeed, he was splendid.

**Man** (*out*)   Look at her! You believe this?

**Woman**   Of course they do. *But* . . . I became lovers with the painter. He wasn't much good – in bed, I mean. 'I know I'm unworthy of you,' he said, 'that my touch is unworthy of you, that when I crawl on you like a spider in the night, my boney fingers trembling on your perfect breasts . . .'

**Man** (*to* **Woman**)   Nobody talks like that!

**Woman**   *He* did . . . 'and when you let me enter in, it is in an act of mercy . . .'

**Man** (*out*)   Nobody! Nobody has *ever* talked like that! (*To* **Boy** *and* **Girl**.) Nobody. EVER. Don't just stand there with your mouths open! Learn something!

**Woman**   'I know all this and I am strengthened by my weakness.' And so on and so forth. And, well, he *was* strengthened; his talent surged; his drawings of me – *and* the paintings – made him, well . . . quite famous. I hang in museums. You didn't know that, *did* you?

**Man** (*in*)   You do not. (*Out.*) She does not. (*To* **Boy** *and* **Girl**.) She does not.

**Woman**   I do not? But I began to see something: that *he* was getting far more out of this than *I* was: he had his lovely decoration, plus a model for free, plus a source of income, and *I* was saddled with this . . . skimpy little man with only bones and drive and the oddest breath and . . . and I felt *tricked*. I be*longed* with the polo players and such, the healthy animals.

**Man** (*back in. Sarcastic*)   Of course you did!

**Woman**   I was young and fabulous.

**Man** (*ibid*)   Yes! Of course you were!

**Woman**   And I suddenly knew that I hadn't gained the days, but I'd merely lost the nights. Do you understand? (*Waits; he merely shakes his head.*) Where was I?

**Man**   Not gained the days but merely lost the nights, or some such rubbish.

**Woman**   . . . Not gained the days but merely lost the nights. And so I broke it off. 'You're using me,' I shrieked at him, pacing his studio, knocking things over. 'You don't love *me*; you love the *fact* of me.' (*Shakes her head.*) Who did I think I was? Who did we *all* think we were? 'I can't live without you,' he called to me from his window as I flounced from the building. 'I'll kill myself!' 'Hanh!' I said, and turned on my heel and . . . vanished into the mist, or whatever. And of course he *did*: kill himself, that is. He hanged himself in his atelier, from a rafter. (*Pause.*) And how does all *that* strike you? How and where does all *that* grab you?

**Man** (*shakes his head; smiles, applauds*)   Very good! Really, very good! (*Out.*) Wasn't that good? Didn't she do that well? Come on, give her a hand! (*Encourages, leads audience applause. She curtsies. If there is none, he dismisses audience with a wave of his hand.*) Good. Really very good. (*To* **Boy** *and* **Girl**.) Didn't you think so? (*Before they can reply: a sudden shift to very businesslike; in.*) Okay. Let's get on with it. (*To* **Boy** *and* **Girl**; *calling.*) Will you two come over here, please? (*Flat.*) What?

**Boy** (*flat*)   What? What is it?

**Man**   Did you like our little performance? Our intermezzo a due? (*Before they can answer.*) Ah! But where's baby-poo?

**Boy** (*flat*)   Asleep; all fed.

**Man** (*licks lips*)   I got dessert.

**Woman** (*false hearty*)   Oh, you have a baby!

**Boy**   Yes.

**Woman**   What kind?

**Boy** (*eyeing her*)   A small one.

**Woman**   A*ha*. (*Exits left; false stealth.*)

**Boy** (*to* **Man**)   What do you want?

**Man** (*cheerless smile*)   What do we *want*. Well, I would
imagine we want what almost everybody wants – eternal
life, in great health, no older than we are when we want it;
easy money, with enough self-deception to make us feel
we've earned it, are worthy people; a government that lets
us do whatever we want, serves our private interests and lets
us feel we're doing all we can for . . . how do they call it –
the less fortunate? a bigger dick, a more muscular vagina; a
baby, perhaps?

**Boy**   No, no. (*Articulated.*) What do you want?

**Man**   Hm?

**Boy**   *Here*; what do you want *here*?

**Man** (*helpless gesture; false*)   I'm not sure that I . . .

**Boy**   You're *here*.

**Man** (*grudging*)   Yes.

**Boy**   That . . . woman is here – is with you.

**Man**   Everything being relative . . .

**Boy**   Yes.

**Girl** (*suspicious*)   Where *is* she? Where's she gone!?
(**Woman** *re-enters, from stage right, very casually, an okay figure
gesture to* **Man**, *a broad wink to him.*) Oh, *there* she is.

**Man** (*to* **Boy**)   We are both here; yes.

**Boy** (*level*)   Why?

**Man**   Hm?

**Boy** (*still level, if harder*)   Why are you here? What do you
want?

**Man** (*cheerless smile*)    What do we *want*. Well, it's really very simple. We've come to take the baby.

*Silence.*

**Boy**    What do you mean!?

**Man** (*flat*)    We've come to take the baby.

*Shorter silence.*

**Girl** (*a look of panic*)    What do you mean 'you've come to take . . .' Oh, my *God*! (*Suddenly exits, left.*)

**Boy** (*eyes on* **Man***; steely*)    I don't understand you.

**Woman**    He doesn't understand you; be clearer.

**Man** (*to* **Woman**)    I thought I was being clear. (*To* **Boy**.) What is it you don't understand? The noun 'baby'? The verb 'take'?

**Woman**    You're not being nice.

**Man**    You told me to be clear – clearer.

**Woman**    They're not mutually exclusive.

**Man** (*heavy sigh*)    *All* right. (*To* **Boy**.) The baby. The baby?

**Boy** (*very innocent*)    Yes?

**Man** (*demonstrates*)    We've come to take it.

**Boy**    I don't . . .

**Man** (*very explicit*)    A-way; a-way.

**Girl** (*re-enters from left; hysterical*)    WHERE'S THE BABY?! WHAT HAVE YOU DONE WITH THE BABY?!

*Silence.*

**Man**    *What* baby?

*Silence.*

**Woman**    Yes; what baby?

*Tableau.*

# Act Two

*No one on-stage; otherwise everything as it was at the end of Act One.*

**Man** (*enters, waves a little to audience. To someone*)   Is this where I was at the end of one – Act One? Right about here? (*Takes exact position as of the end of Act One. Generally; out.*) Yes? Good. (*To stragglers.*) Hurry back in, now; you don't want to miss the exposition. Well, maybe you do. (*Irritated complaint.*) '*Honestly*! You'd think they'd have it in the *first* act!' (*Thinks about it.*) No; you couldn't possibly. Well, let me tell you: intermissions are never long enough, are they. Did you enjoy yourselves while you were out for your cigarettes, or whatever? (*Wrinkles his nose, etc.*) Don't smoke; bad for you. Half a million die of it every year. In this country alone, subsidized murder. Not *you*, of course – someone you know. So; you had your cigarette, or your drink – not *quite* so bad, one or two a day good for the old heart, they say. *Or* your coffee. (*Harpy; shrill.*) KEEP AWAKE! KEEP AWAKE! Or merely . . . stretching your legs, having a pee. (*Annoyed woman imitation.*) 'You'd think they'd build the ladies' restrooms bigger; after all these years you'd think they'd have noticed the lines! *Honestly!*' Or maybe just a phone call? Or a talk with friends – *or* strangers. Whatever. (*Shift of tone.*) I must tell you something here: I have a troubling sense of what should be – rather than what *is*. It chokes me up at simple-minded movies – where good things happen to good people? My throat clots, and I think I'm going to cry. Because I know it can never happen in what they call 'real life'? Good things to good people and happy endings? That it's all . . . fantasy? Is that what allows me to believe? To weep in relief? If I saw it *really* happening – all good things to all good people? – would I turn away in horror? Yes, probably: because it could all . . . stop, could go away, be a single instant of glory, desperately cruel. We can't take glory because it shows us the abyss. That is why we cry at movies – because it's *safe* to; it's all so . . . beautifully false. But I have, as I say, this sense of what should be rather than what is. And I file it

away; file it away under 'unwanted on the voyage,
dangerous cargo,' for I know it does not apply? Because it is
an impediment to . . . what do they say? . . . to 'getting
through it all'? (*Smiles grimly; demonstrates shuddering.*) It's
troubling, though, I *tell* you. As . . . (*gestures*) . . . as in, well
. . . *here*; now; all this. Troubling, but I'll get through it.
(*Snaps fingers.*) Okay!! So, where did we leave off? 'We've
come to take the baby.' 'I don't understand.' 'What baby?'
etc. That was it . . . casual – more or less – straightforward,
but casual. 'We've come to take the baby.' Remember it?
Good. We'll see if they let us take the baby from then. (*In.*)
Where were we all? (*Off.*) Will you come back in now? (**Boy**
*and* **Girl** *re-enter from left,* **Women** *from right; they take positions
identical to their positions on* **Man***'s 'Okay. Let's get on with it.'*)
Fine. (*To* **Boy** *and* **Girl**.) Now you two say 'What?', 'What is
it?' You first, then her, flat, flat, both of you. Say it! 'What?'
'What is it?' (*Pause.*) Say it, for God's sake!

**Boy** ( *flat*)    What?

**Girl** ( *flat*)    What? What is it?

**Man** (*approving*)    That's right; that's it. (*False hearty.*) Good
to see you! But where's 'the little one?'

**Girl** ( *flat*)    Asleep; all fed.

**Boy** (*licks lips*)    I got dessert.

**Woman** (*quiet aside to* **Man**)    Oh, I get it. (*To* **Girl***; false
hearty.*) Oh, you have a baby!

**Girl**    Yes.

**Woman**    What kind?

**Girl** (*eyeing her*)    A small one.

**Woman**    Aha. (*Quick aside to* **Man**.) Is this where I . . .
(*answering her own question*) . . . yes; yes, it is. (*To* **Girl**.) Aha!
(*Exits left; false stealthy.*)

**Boy** (*to* **Man**)    What do you want?

**Man** (*sotto voce aside to audience*)   I love this speech. (*To* **Boy**; *cheerless smile.*) What do we *want*. Well, I would imagine we want what almost everybody wants – eternal life, in great health, no older than we are when we want it; easy money, with enough self-deception to make us feel we've earned it, are worthy people; a government that lets us do whatever we want, serves our private interests and lets us feel we're doing all we can for . . . how do they call it – the less fortunate? a bigger dick, a more muscular vagina; a baby, perhaps?

**Boy**   No, no. (*Articulated.*) What do you *want*?

**Man**   Hm?

**Boy**   *Here*; what do you want *here*?

**Man** (*helpless gesture; false*)   I'm not sure that I . . .

**Boy**   You're *here*.

**Man** (*grudging*)   Yes.

**Boy**   That . . . woman is here – is with you.

**Man**   Everything being relative . . .

**Boy**   Yes.

**Girl** (*suspicious*)   Where is she? Where's she *gone*!? (**Women** *re-enters, from stage right, very casually, an okay finger gesture to* **Man**, *with a broad wink.*) Oh, *there* she is.

**Man** (*to* **Boy**)   We are both here; yes.

**Boy** (*level*)   Why?

**Man**   Hm?

**Boy** (*still level, if harder*)   Why are you here? What do you want?

**Man** (*cheerless smile*)   What do we *want*. Well, it's really very simple. We've come to take the baby.

*Silence.*

**Man** (*flat*)    We've come to take the baby.

*Shorter silence.*

**Girl** (*a look of panic*)    What do you mean 'you've come to take . . .' Oh, my God! (*Suddenly exits, left.*)

**Boy** (*eyes on* **Man***; steely*)    I don't understand you. (*Brief awareness of* **Girl***'s action.*)

**Woman**    He doesn't understand you; be clearer.

**Man** (*to* **Woman**)    I thought I was being clear. (*To* **Boy**.) What is it you don't understand? The noun 'baby'? The verb 'take'?

**Woman**    You're not being nice.

**Man**    You told me to be clear – clearer.

**Woman**    They're not mutually exclusive.

**Man** (*heavy sigh*)    *All* right. (*To* **Boy**.) The baby. The baby?

**Boy** (*very innocent*)    Yes?

**Man** (*demonstrates*)    We've come to take it.

**Boy**    I don't . . .

**Man** (*very explicit; impatient*)    A-way; a-way.

**Girl** (*re-enters from left; hysterical*)    WHERE'S THE BABY?! WHAT HAVE YOU DONE WITH THE BABY?!

*Silence.*

**Man**    *What* baby?

*Silence.*

**Woman**    Yes; *what* baby?

**Man** (*out, then in*)    *There* we are! *Here* we go!

**Girl**    WHAT HAVE YOU DONE WITH MY BABY??!!

**Boy** (*gathering energy; clearly about to lunge*)    Look, you motherfucker, what have you done to . . .

**Man** (*a stopping hand up; very loud*)   STOP!! (**Boy** *freezes*.)

**Girl** (*sobbing*)   What have you done with my baby?

**Man** (*loud*)   BOTH OF YOU!! NOW JUST STOP!!

**Girl** *whimpers, sobs, but stays still;* **Boy** *puts his arm around her, never taking his eyes off* **Man**.

**Woman** (*distaste*)   Such a performance! You'd think somebody was hurting somebody – or something!

**Man** (*keeping his eyes on* **Boy***; casual tone*)   Wouldn't you?

**Woman**   You'd think something was amiss, as they say.

**Man** (*ibid*)   Wouldn't you?

**Girl** (*weepy*)   I want my baby.

**Man**   *Everyone* wants his baby.

**Woman**   *Her* baby.

**Man** (*shrugs*)   Whatever. (*To* **Woman***; points at* **Girl** *innocence*.) *Her* baby? Everyone wants her baby?

**Woman** (*chuckles*)   No, no; generics again.

**Boy** (*about to get up, move towards* **Man**)   Okay. I've had enough of this now! What the fuck have you done with . . .

**Man** (*hand up*)   Hold!

**Boy** (*beginning to move*)   I will not 'hold,' whatever that means.

**Woman** (*helpful*)   It's Elizabethan.

**Boy** (*confused*)   It's . . . it's *what*?!

**Man**   ELIZABETHAN!! Now go sit down. If you care about this baby you behave yourself, yourselves. (*Demonstrates*.) If there are two hands – see? two hands? – if there are two hands, we have the upper one. If you have ever had a baby –

**Boy**   If?

**Man**  . . . if that is mother's milk you've been feeding on, and if you wish to see your real or imagined baby again – ever! –

**Boy**   Real? Or . . .

**Man**  . . . if you are wiser than your years, be good.

**Boy** *does so.*

**Woman** (*To* **Man**)   You have a way with children.

**Man**   As it was with my own.

**Woman**   Oh? You have children?

**Man**   Certainly; I have six.

**Woman**   Really!

**Man**   Yes: two black, two white, one green, and the other . . . well, I'm not certain, or I've lost track, or whatever.

**Boy** (*quietly*)   Bullshit.

**Woman** (*ignoring* **Boy**)   Two black?

**Man**   Yes.

**Woman**   Half black, half white, what in the bad old days they used to call mulatto?

**Man**   No; all black.

**Woman**   But . . .

**Man**   This was when I was black.

**Woman**   A*ha*. Was this before you were white? Before . . .

**Man**   No; it shifted: two white, one black, one green, etc.

**Woman**   I see; I see.

**Girl** (*to* **Man**)   You have no children.

**Man**   Well, that may be, or may have been, or . . . whatever.

**Woman** (*to* **Girl**)   Why do you say that?

**Girl** (*to* **Woman**)   Nor do you.

**Woman**   Oh?

**Girl**   No one who has children . . .

**Man**   Had!

**Girl** (*onward*)   . . . would treat us like this – anyone like this

**Boy**   She's right, you know. (*Pause.*) Had?

**Man** (*playful*)   Well, *having* had doesn't mean one *has*. (*Pause.*) Does it?

**Woman**   One green?

**Man**   Yes. (*Out.*) Does this need explaining?

**Woman**   When you were green?

**Man** (*back in; thinks a moment*)   Well, when *some*one was.

**Woman**   Half green then.

**Girl** (*soft, gentle pleading*)   Please? (**Boy** *quietly shushes her.*)

**Man** (*considers it*)   Mmmmm . . . light green. (*To* **Boy** *and* **Girl**.) So, I want you to understand I know about children, about who has them . . . and who does *not*; how large they may be, how many legs they have – if they have the number they are supposed to, where they come out of – the length of the small intestine in a two-week-old . . .

**Woman**   How long?

**Man**   Eleven and three-quarter inches. The color of loss, the names most commonly not used . . . all the things essential. You don't fool with *me*. Fool yourselves, fool each *other*, but don't try it with *me*. *I've* touched the golden dick. Have *you*? (*To* **Boy**, *specifically*.) *Have* you? Have you? You there?

**Boy** (*preoccupied*)   Have I what?

**Man**   Touched the golden dick.

**Boy**   I don't know what you're talking about, mister. (*Suddenly loud.*) Where's our baby!!??

**Man/Woman** (*softly singing*)   Yes, sir, where's our baby? No, sir, we don't mean maybe. Yes, sir, where's our baby now?

**Man** (*speaking again*)   Too bad about the dick – the golden dick. (*As* **Boy** *prepares to lunge.*) I'd be careful if I were you!)

**Boy** *lunges;* **Man** *flips him on his back on the floor with a judo move; pins* **Boy**'s *neck under his foot.*

**Man**   I said I'd be careful if I were you! (*To* **Girl**.) Are you going to try something, too? (**Girl** *sobs, shakes her head.*) Good; the lady here is adept at things as well.

**Woman**   I am.

**Man**   Everyone's adept at something. (*To pinned* **Boy**.) Will you be good?

**Boy**   Yes.

**Man**   Good. (**Boy** *gets us, not easily.*) Go to your chair. (**Boy** *Does;* **Girl** *moves to comfort him.*) Good. Touching. (*To* **Woman**.) Goodness, I'm saying 'good' a lot, *aren't* I?

**Woman** (*shrugs*)   It *sounds* right.

**Man**   Good! (*To* **Boy** *and* **Girl**.) So! No more shenanigans. (*Out.*) Is that Irish? Shenanigans? (*If anyone answers, handle it; in any event, go on with this.*) I looked it up once in the dictionary and it didn't say; it said 'informal,' which I don't believe is a genesis. Though maybe it is . . . the island of informality? The city of shenanigan? I meant to look it up somewhere else, but I . . . lost interest, I guess. (*Back in.*) In any event, (*to* **Boy** *and* **Girl**) no more (*very pronounced*) she-nan-igans. No?

**Boy** (*nursing his neck*)   No.

**Man**   No what?

**Boy**   No more.

**Man**   No more *what*!?

**Boy**   No more shenanigans.

**Man**   Always be precise: saves time, saves paper. Did I hurt you?

**Boy**   No.

**Man**   No wound?

**Boy**   No.

**Man** (*to* **Boy** *and* **Girl**)   If you have no wounds, how can you know if you're alive? If you have no scar, how do you know who you are? Have been?

**Boy** (*impatient*)   Come on, mister!

**Woman** (*to* **Boy**)   Listen to him.

**Man** (*to* **Boy**)   Was your fracture compound? Did it stick out through the skin – like snapped wood?

**Girl** (*to* **Boy**, *shy*)   *Did* it?

**Boy**   No!

**Man**   If it didn't, who *are* you! Who *have* you ever *been*? (*To* **Girl**.) Was it a caesarean for the baby? A theoretical caesarean for the theoretical baby?

**Boy**   Theor . . .

**Girl**   No! No wound!

**Man** (*to them both*)   Blood? Piercings? Gougings? Wounds, children, wounds. Without wounds what *are* you? You're too young for the batterings time brings us . . .

**Woman** (*dramatic*)   Oh, God! The batterings!

**Man** (*to* **Woman**)   . . . time brings us.

**Woman**   Sorry! . . . time brings us. (*An aside.*) Oh, God?

**Man**    One is enough. (*To* **Boy**.) Give me your arm; let me see your wound.

**Boy** (*self-protective*)    Hah! You think I'd fall for that!?

**Man**    Oh, I wouldn't break your arm; I don't want you on your knees – not literally. Ever? No, I don't think so. Break your arm? Nahhhh! Your heart, perhaps. Your heart, yes. Certainly your heart.

**Woman** (*pleased*)    Oh, the heart!

**Man**    Give me your heart, then; I'll break *that*. If you don't have the wound of a broken heart, how can you know you're alive? If you have no broken heart, how do you know who you are? Have been? Can ever be?

**Girl** (*to* **Man** *and* **Woman***; crying a little*)    Leave us alone? Please, let me have my baby?

**Man** (*sighs*)    We're going to have to talk about this. (*Beginning of lecture?*) What is a baby? (*Out.*) What is a baby? (*In and out, now.*) We must, first of all, define a baby. A baby . . . *what*!? A baby mouse?, a baby kangaroo?, a baby wolverine?, a baby . . . *baby*. A human baby, an almost, not quite yet human baby – no larger than, well, somewhat larger than that 'great divide'. (*To* **Boy**.) Hey? Between the something slopes, or something?

**Boy** (*curt*)    What?

**Man**    Nothing. (*In and out again.*) You can't go home again? Surely not! They say we want to go back in – back home – some of us, at any rate. Try it! A minute after out-you-slide – or whatever – it's all closing up, closing down, 'till the next time. Push you back in – head first, whatever? Wouldn't work! The water's gone now; you've been shocked into breathing . . . what?, nothing *you* can see, *could* see if you had *eyes* – eyes that *opened*. (*Bravura quote.*) 'Oh, blessed eyes that never ope!' (*Natural again.*) 'Ope'; I've always liked 'ope.'

**Woman** (*matter-of-fact*)    You're running on.

**Man**   Yes? I am?

**Woman**   'What is a baby?' Then relate *that* to where we are – to this.

**Man**   Aha!

**Girl** (*quiet*)   Please? My baby?

**Man** (*hearty*)   Now, look; if there *is* a baby, and if it is yours, and you can prove it's yours, we'll handle it.

**Boy** (*ominously quiet*)   If? Who *are* you? Who are you, really?

**Girl**   Yes; who *are* you?

**Man** (*to* **Boy**)   I am your destination. Remember? Is that familiar? (*To* **Woman**.) Now you.

**Woman** (*tiny orienting pause; to* **Girl**)   Yes. Yes, I go in the back with you, and I am your destination.

**Man** (*to* **Boy**)   We do things together, you and I, that no one else has done.

**Woman** (*to* **Girl**)   You love me; we are each other's . . . whatever.

**Girl** (*intense; to* **Boy**)   None of this is true!

**Man** (*to* **Boy**)   The first time you touched me . . . (*indicates*) there, I almost fainted. It was so . . . unexpected, I suppose.

**Boy** (*cold*)   You fuck!

**Man** (*considers*)   Well . . . yes.

**Woman** (*to* **Girl***; dreamy*)   We lay there, you and I, true spoons, the two of us, mouths on each other . . .

**Girl** (*voice shaking*)   No! No!

**Man** (*to* **Boy**)   We are each other's destination. No? Yes?

**Woman** (*to* **Girl**)   No? We are not?

**Man** (*to both* **Boy** *and* **Girl**)   Or are we Gypsies? Hm?

**Girl** (*to* **Boy***; hysterical*)    They're Gypsies!!

**Boy** (*eyes on* **Man***; steely, to comfort*)    No; no, they're not.

**Man** (*pretending bewilderment*)    We're *not*!?

**Boy**    No!

**Man** (*of* **Woman**)    You don't recognize her fedora and her huge mustache?

**Woman** (*to* **Girl**)    You came to me; you brought your life savings in a paper bag.

**Girl**    No! I don't *have* any life savings!

**Boy** (*pleading; explaining*)    We're very young.

**Man**    And therefore you don't have Gypsies? (*To* **Girl**.) *She* had a Gypsy.

**Woman** (*to* **Girl**)    Yes, you *went* to one. (*Uncertain.*) Was it *me*? Was it to me?

**Boy**    But it wasn't for *that*.

**Man**    For *what*.

**Girl**    For . . . life savings, and all.

**Man**    Well, I should hope not. How dumb can you be?!

**Woman** (*to* **Man***, about* **Girl**)    That's for *later*, when you *get* dumb, life-savings-time dumb.

**Man** (*sighs*)    Time; time, the great leveler. (*To* **Boy***; sweet.*) Tell me *about* you; tell us your history. (*Whispered aside; out.*) Exposition.

**Boy** (*confused*)    Who? Me?

**Man** (*back in*)    Whatever. You can tell us your history, or she can tell us your history, and you can tell us hers, and we won't know *what* to disbelieve.

**Boy** (*a recitation; quiet rage*)    I'm a twenty-three-year-old white, Anglo-Saxon American man . . .

**Man**   That's a redundancy. All Anglo-Saxons are white.

**Boy**   Yes? A twenty-three-year-old Anglo-Saxon American man . . .

**Man**   Boy.

**Boy**   Boy – yes? – boy, and I'm married to *her*, the light of my life.

**Woman**   Your destination.

**Boy** (*confused*)   What?

**Woman** (*cheerful*)   Your destination! Don't you remember?

**Man** (*to* **Boy**)   I thought it was you and me: that time you touched me . . . (*gestures*) here, and put your lips to my . . .

**Boy** (*loud enough to cover*)   THE LIGHT OF MY LIFE!

**Man/Woman** (*as if on cue*)
   Roll me over, in the clover,
   Roll me over, lay me down, and do it again.

**Man** (*to* **Boy** *and* **Girl**)   Familiar? No?

**Boy** (*shaking his head*)   What more do you want? When will you . . .

**Man** (*expansive*)   Ohhhhh, *much* more.

**Girl** (*sudden*)   I want my baby!

**Woman** (*groucho*)   Everybody wants his baby – her baby – whatever.

**Man** (*to* **Boy**)   Tell us more; tell us what we want to know, and then tell us what we *don't*. I'd like to know for example, why you took up with this young woman, when you obviously despise her.

**Boy** (*rage; frustration*)   I *love* her; I love her with all my *heart*!

**Woman** (*to* **Man**; *false support of* **Boy**)   He *loves* her, she loves *him*.

**Boy**   YES!!

**Man**   Tisk, tisk, tisk! Then, what shall I think of the letter you sent me when we were apart . . .

**Boy**   We were never together!

**Man**   . . . when we were apart, saying it was all for show, that her family has money, you can't stand the smell of her, the things she makes you do, and . . .

**Boy** (*making to lunge*)   You motherfucking . . . !!

**Man** (*warning hand up instantly*)   Hanh!! The baby? Remember the baby?

**Boy**   Lady . . .

**Woman**   You said you would paint me . . . naked, my lovely breasts, the dimple of my belly, my milk-pink hips, my burning bush?

**Girl** *begins to weep*.

**Man** (*scoffing*)   Milk-pink?

**Woman** (*a trifle defensive*)   Well . . . yes. (*To* **Boy**.) You were only one of my lovers, of course, one of the sturdy, virile boys, the young and handsome, well-muscled . . .

**Girl** (*to* **Boy**; *rage and tears*)   You know her!!

**Boy** (*trying to comfort her; dogmatic*)   No! No, I don't know her!

**Man** (*to no one*)   Oh what a wangled teb we weave.

**Woman**   A what?

**Man**   a teb; a wangled teb.

**Woman**   What is *that*?

**Man**   *You* remember. He was only one of your lovers, no?

**Woman**   Hm! Oh! Oh; right. (*To* **Boy**.) You were a *splendid* lover, though . . . slow, patient, thoughtful, but always in command, and driving . . .

**Girl** (*to* **Boy**; *still weeping*)   You *know* her!

**Boy** (*pounding his fists on his knees*)   I do *not*! I do *not* know her!

**Man** (*to* **Woman**, *but so* **Girl** *will hear*)   When *was* all this? When were you two lovers?

**Woman** (*with a toss of her hand*)   Oh . . . last year, last month, last week, on his way to seeing her at the hospital, on his way from seeing her at the hospital – her and the baby. Earlier today.

**Man**   To so-called baby.

**Woman** (*smiles*)   The so-called baby.

**Boy** (*quiet intensity; almost crying*)   I don't know you! I've never been with anyone but her.

**Man** (*to* **Woman**)   Tell me about his penis; compare notes, so to speak. Show her you know the man through his manhood.

**Boy** (*flustered rage*)   She's never seen my penis!

**Woman** (*about to begin*)   Well, all right now, let me see: I've seen penie in my life, and on a scale of one to ten – ten being *very* un*likely* – I would says that he was a . . . oh, a . . .

**Girl** (*exuberant in her invention*)   He doesn't have one! She couldn't have seen it because he doesn't have one! So there!!

**Boy** (**Girl** *nudges him*)   Right! She's right! So there!

**Girl**   So there! (*Giggles.*)

**Man** (*out*)   They are so in*ven*tive, these two. (*Back in; to* **Boy** *and* **Girl**.) In the sense that the Queen of Spain does not have legs?

**Boy** (*cold*)   What?

**Man** (*out; pleasant*)   It is said that once, centuries ago, an envoy from the East came to the Spanish court – with gifts, of course, gifts for the royal family; including fine-spun silk, a novelty back then. 'For her Majesty,' the envoy said, in his

– well, his silkiest tone. (**Woman** *chuckles appreciatively*.)
Thank you. 'For her Majesty, silk for her Majesty's legs.'
The major domo – or whatever he was – their Majesty's
major-domo, sniffed, the story goes, raised his eyebrows at
the effrontery, the familiarity, and said, in his haughtiest
tone, 'The Queen of Spain does not have . . . legs.' (*Back in;
to* **Boy** *and* **Girl**.) Is that the sense you mean, that your
young man does not have a penis in the sense that the
Queen of Spain does not have legs? Or are we dealing here
with a bewildering and somber deformity, one which puts
into even greater question the matter of a baby?

**Woman** (*rather puzzled*)    That's something you'd think I
would have noticed – or not noticed, rather.

**Boy** (*pause*)    Go fuck yourselves.

**Man**    Right on! (*He and* **Woman** *slap each other's right palms.*
**Girl** *tries to sneak off, with an 'it's okay' gesture to* **Boy**. **Man**
*notices; a warning.*) I wouldn't do that!!! (**Girl** *hesitates*.) Leave
the so-called baby be! *If* you have a baby –

**Boy**    I told you, we have a baby.

**Girl**    Yes, we have a baby

**Man**    . . . If there *is* a baby, who is to say it has ever been
yours? Who is to say you have a right to it? Or that you
didn't steal it? Gypsies *do* steal things.

**Woman**    Yes; yes, they do.

**Man** (*to* **Girl**; *very harsh*)    So . . . SIDDDOWN!!

**Girl** (*sitting; weeping quietly*)    We are not Gypsies.

**Boy** (*will this help?*)    No; no, we're not.

**Woman**    Well . . . *some*one is.

**Man** (*seemingly puzzled*)    Yes; yes, that's right . . . *some*one is,
*must* be. (*To* **Girl**; *steely*.) If you can prove it is yours –
belongs to you . . . you did not steal it, as Gypsies do . . .
belongs to *you* . . .

**Woman** (*helping*)   . . . and belongs *with* you . . .

**Man** (*to* **Woman**)   Yes; right; thank you.

**Woman**   Welcome.

**Girl**   I *told* you . . .

**Boy**   She *told* you . . .

**Man** (*to* **Girl** *again*)   . . . Belongs to you, *and* belongs *with* you, then your interest in seeing it *ever* transcends your need to see it now. (*Pause.*) No?

**Girl** (*still quietly weeping*)   Yes; yes, it does.

**Man**   Good girl; you'll go far – to paraphrase.

**Boy**   I'll ask you one more time, mister, and only once more, who do you . . .

**Man** (*to* **Boy** *and* **Girl**)   No; the question is not who I think I am, but who I cannot be – the knowledge we all have of who we all cannot be, singularly, of course. I've lived long enough to understand that *that* is the most important question. Keep it in mind as you go on through it – both of you: what we cannot do; who we cannot be.

**Woman** *begins signing – clearly absurd signing-like gestures.*

**Man**   *What* are you doing?

**Woman**   Signing

**Man**   You know *how*? You know how to *sign*?

**Woman** (*signing*)   It would seem so.

**Man**   When did you learn? And *why*? *Why* did you learn?

**Woman** (*shrugs; signs*)   It came upon me.

**Man**   When?

**Woman**   Just now; I just realized I could do it.

**Man**   Sign away.

**Woman** (*signing; smiling*)    Thank you.

**Man** (*out now*)    Ignore her; I mean pay attention if you want to, but concentrate on *me*. *I* am talking; she is listening. Well, she is talking, too, in a way, but following *me*. She listens and then talks, almost simultaneously, but not quite. I . . . *talk*. I even listen as I *talk* – to myself, not to her. I can't sign. (**Woman** *stops signing*.) You've stopped.

**Woman**    It comes and goes. I've suddenly forgotten. You go on; I'll catch up.

**Man** (*scoffs*)    With me? Never! (*Out again*.) So. Who I cannot be. (*To* **Boy** *and* **Girl**.) Learn from this, children. (*Out again*.) I cannot be young again; I cannot be a woman therefore I cannot have babies, blah, blah, blah, if indeed I *would* have them, or *could*. (*To* **Girl**.) Eh, toots?

**Girl**    Leave me alone!

**Boy** (*gentle pleading*)    Leave her alone.

**Man** (*to* **Girl**)    But you *asked* . . . or he did: who I thought I was, etcetera. (*In and out now*.) I would like, above all else, to be . . . historical and free-floating; I regret the people I have not met. I regret Jesus most of all. Still: to *really* . . . *hear* him. (*To* **Boy** *and* **Girl**, *who just look back*.) How many sentences do the scholars think are his in the testaments? Three? A half-dozen? (*Dismissive gesture; back out*.) No education. To have *been* there; to have heard him speak. (*To* **Woman**.) This is important.

**Woman**    I know, I know; I'll try. (*Begins signing again, badly, then better*.)

**Man** (*in and out again; ecstatic*)    The Sermon on the Mount! Oh, my God! One could dine out on that . . . *forever*! The truth about the Last Supper? I almost don't dare mention the Crucifixion! Would I have tried to stop it? Would He have made me *not*? Not tried? Was it what he wanted? The proof he needed?

**Woman** (*stops signing*)    You go too far!

**Man** (*apologetic*)   I know, I know; madness lies that way.

**Girl** (*quiet begging*)   Please?

**Man** (*to* **Girl**)   Soon; soon, now. (*To himself, mostly; shakes head.*) All the things I know I can never be, can never do, can never . . . *un*do. That's the worst. (*Ponders.*) All the things I can never be (*harsher now, to* **Boy** *and* **Girl**), including as sympathetic as you would like to your . . . what? – your 'plight'? Your supposed *plight*? You who are probably not what you say you are – *who* you say you are.

**Boy** (*weary*)   I've told you . . . a hundred times . . .

**Man**   Yes, yes, yes, I know; you're married – to one another . . . you have this baby.

**Boy**   Yes!

**Girl**   Yes!

**Man** (*dismissive*)   Right; sure; and the Gypsies have taken it – or will, or have thought about it, at the very least, as Gypsies will.

**Girl** *weeps;* **Boy** *takes her hand.*

**Boy** (*very serious; very calm*)   The baby is real; the baby is ours; we went to the hospital for her to have it. (**Girl** *nods, still weeping a little.*)

**Woman**   You go to the hospital a *lot.*

**Man** (*remembering*)   Yes! Yes, you do! You came to *see* me; I was on the stretcher; I was unconscious . . .

**Woman** (*to* **Man***; of* **Boy**)   . . . and he said to himself: 'When he wakes up – *if* he wakes up – I'm going to be there . . .'

**Man**   '. . . and I'll be the first person he sees, and he'll love me; he'll want me and he'll love me; he's my destination.'

**Woman**   And he told them he was your brother.

**Man** (*to* **Boy**)   And I woke up, and you were hard.

**Girl**    It was me!

**Boy**    It was her!

**Girl**    It was me!

**Man** (*pause*)    Oh?

**Woman** (*pause*)    Oh?

**Boy** (*dogged; almost in tears*)    Yes; yes. It was her; she woke up and I was hard.

**Man** (*surprise*)    It wasn't me?! *I* remember you being hard.

**Woman** (*to* **Boy**)    We all do; we all remember you being hard.

**Man**    Dick or no.

**Woman**    Dick or no.

**Man**    and out popped the baby, the so-called baby?

**Boy**    When?

**Man**    Then!

**Woman**    *When*-then.

**Boy**    No; that was when we *met*!

**Man**    I remember; I woke up; the nurse said you were my brother, and you were hard.

**Boy** (*more dogged*)    No! Not then then; not that time! When we went to have the baby!

**Man** (*distant*)    I don't remember. Was it me? I don't remember.

**Woman**    Maybe it was *me*.

**Boy** (*to prove his existence;* **Girl** *cries softly during this*)    I was in the kitchen, and she came in and she said, 'My water broke; my water just broke!'

**Woman**    It *was* me! Yes; of course.

**Boy**    And I bundled her up, and we took a cab to the hospital. I called our baby doctor, and we raced off to the hospital.

**Man** (*shakes his head*)    Everyone's a baby – even the doctor.

**Woman** (*to* **Boy**)    It isn't *water*, you know. (*To* **Girl**.) It isn't water.

**Boy** (*determined*)    . . . And it wasn't long; it didn't take very long.

**Man** (*remembering giving birth*)    But it hurt! Oh, my God, it hurt! How it hurt me!

**Woman** (*remembering*)    Oh, God, how it hurt me!

**Boy** (*ibid*)    And I held her hand during it, and *I* squeezed and *she* squeezed . . .

**Girl** *begins howling birthing sounds now, punctuating* **Boy**'s *speech; she stays seated; shows no emotion, hands in lap – merely howling.*

**Boy**    . . . and she howled . . . and she howled . . . and she howled . . . and the sound was terrible, but I held on, *we* held on . . . the doctor and the nurses were all there . . . and the blood . . . and the blood came, and I'd never seen so much . . . blood, and then the baby came, the baby's head came (**Girl** *ceases howling*) . . . and the rest of it . . .

**Girl** (*hands going wide*)    WOOOOOOSSSSSSH!!

**Man** (*ecstasy*)    . . . and I'd never seen so much blood!

**Woman** (*ecstasy*)    . . . I felt it! The blood, and then the baby . . .

**Boy** (*ignoring them; maybe with a dismissive hand gesture*)    . . . and there it was; there was our baby.

**Girl** (*softer*)    Wooooosssssh.

**Woman** (*shakes her head*)    Just like in the movies.

**Man** (*agreeing; suddenly understanding*)    Yes! (*To* **Boy**.) You go to a lot of movies?

**Boy** (*bewildered*)    Who? This wasn't a movie!

**Woman**    It looked like one to *me* – all the trappings.

**Man** (*to* **Woman**)    Yes! *Did*n't it? When I had *my* baby . . .

**Woman**    The black one?

**Man**    No; the green one; there was very little blood, no pain . . .

**Woman**    Well, you had a spinal.

**Man**    Hmmmm! Yes, that may have had something to do with it. In any event, when I had *my* baby *I* had the Gypsies, too. The Gypsies came to me, too.

**Woman** (*smiles*)    Too?

**Man** (*smiles*)    Whatever. But I was wise. (*To* **Girl**.) When I took *my* baby to the Gypsy . . .

**Woman**    The old Gypsy *woman*.

**Man** (*aside, to* **Woman**)    Whatever. (*To* **Girl** *again*.) When I took *my* baby to the Gypsy, *I* was smart; when they told me to put the baby in a big paper bag, I didn't *do* it.

**Girl** (*weeping*)    No! I *did*n't!

**Woman** (*to* **Man**)    Of *course* you didn't!

**Man** (*still to* **Girl**)    *I* didn't put it on the table, between me and the Gypsy.

**Woman**    Of course you didn't!

**Man** (*still to* **Girl**)    *I* didn't see the lights go all funny, and hear the music.

**Woman**    Of course not!

**Man** (*still to* **Girl**)    And *I* didn't take the bag and bury it in the back yard for three weeks, so the baby could double, or whatever.

**Woman** (*out*)    Twins!

**Girl**    No! I didn't

**Boy**    She didn't!

**Woman** (*to* **Man**)    Of course you didn't!

**Man**    So that when it came time to dig it up . . .

**Girl** (*weeping*)    I . . . didn't . . . do . . . that!

**Boy** (*comforting her*)    No; no; of course you didn't.

**Woman** (*observing*)    Touching.

**Man**    Or whatever.

**Girl**    Please. My baby.

**Man** (*pause; brisk now*)    Well, time for the old blanket trick.

**Woman**    Oh; right! (*Exiting right; to* **Boy** *and* **Girl**.) I'll be right back. (*Out.*) I'll be right back.

**Man** (*to* **Boy** *and* **Girl**, *as* **Girl** *looks apprehensively off right*) She'll be right back. (*Out.*) She'll be right back.

**Boy** (*after a pause; shy; quietly fearful*)    Are you Gypsies?

**Man** (*laughs; to* **Boy**)    Do we look like Gypsies? Do we have fedoras and bushy mustaches . . . ?

**Boy**    Whatever, then. Have you come to hurt us? Beyond salvation? Hurt us to the point that . . . if you want to do this to us, hurt us so, ask *why*! Ash what we've *done*. I can take pain and loss and all the rest *later*; I *think* I can – *we* can – when it comes as natural as . . . sleep? But . . . now? Not now. We're happy; we love each other; I'm hard all the time; we have a baby; we don't even understand each other yet. So . . . give us some time. (*Pause.*) Please.

**Man** (*after long pause; brisk*)    Time's up.

**Woman** *re-enters with the baby blanket bundle, nuzzling.* **Girl** *instinctively reaches towards bundle.*

**Woman** (*possessive*)    AH!

**Girl** *withdraws.*

**Boy** (*an echo from before*)    Please?

**Man** (*gentler*)   Time's up. (**Woman** *hands him the bundle. Out; a barker.*) Ladies and gentlemen! See what we have here! The baby bundle! The old bundle of baby! (*Throws it up in the air, catches it;* **Girl** *screams.*)

**Boy** (*desperate*)   Don't do *that*!

**Woman** (*to* **Boy***; comforting*)   He knows what he's doing.

**Man** (*to* **Boy** *and* **Girl**)   I know what I'm doing. (*Out again; in when necessary.*) The old baby bundle – treasure of treasures, light of our lives, purpose – they say – of all the fucking, all the . . . well, all the everything. Now the really good part, the part we've all been waiting for! (*He takes the bundle, snaps it open, displays both sides; we see there is nothing there.*) Shazaam! You see? Nothing! No baby! Nothing! (**Girl** *goes to blanket;* **Man** *gives it to her; she searches it, cuddles it; weeps. To* **Girl**.) You see? Nothing.

**Boy** (*pause*)   You *have* decided then: you have decided to hurt us beyond salvation.

**Man** (*objective*)   I said: time's up.

**Boy**   No matter how young we are? No matter how . . .

**Woman** (*gentle*)   He said: time's up.

**Man**   I said: time's up. Wounds, children, wounds. If you have no wounds, how can you know you're alive? How can you know who you are? (**Boy** *bows his head. To* **Boy** *and* **Girl**.) Let us deal finally, once and for all, with the baby – I put it in quotes, 'baby'. I want you to be certain, you have a baby? Have ever *had* a baby. (*Pause.*) You have a baby?

**Girl** *replies more and more tentatively;* **Boy** *stays firm.* (*Don't rush this section.*)

**Boy**   Yes.

**Girl**   Yes.

*Pause.*

**Man**   You have a baby?

**Boy**    Yes.

**Girl**    Yes.

*Pause.*

**Woman**    You have a baby?

**Boy**    Yes.

**Girl**    Yes.

*Pause.*

**Man**    You have a baby?

**Boy**    Yes.

**Girl** *opens mouth; closes it.*

**Boy** (*tiny pause*)    Say something! (*She shakes her head. Increasing intensity, and increased tempo here.*)

**Man**    I'll ask you once again. You have a baby?

**Boy** (*to* **Girl**)    Tell him.

**Girl** (*finally*)    I don't know.

**Boy**    Of course you know!

**Girl**    No! I don't know!

**Man**    Once more: you have a baby?

**Boy** (*to* **Girl**)    *Tell* him!!

**Woman** (*gentle*)    Tell me, too.

**Boy**    *Tell* her!

**Man**    Tell *someone*: you have a baby?

**Girl** (*long pause; finally; rather shy*)    No; I don't think so.

**Boy**    But . . . ?

**Girl** (*to* **Boy**; *begging*)    No; no; we don't have  one; we don't have a baby. (*Varying intensities and tempi.*) Please, please, no baby, I can't . . .

**Boy** (*rage*)   I was with you when it was born!

**Girl** (*flat*)   No.

**Boy**   No one before *me*; we *made* it!

**Man** (*an aside; quiet; out*)   They all say that.

**Girl** (*flat*)   No.

**Boy**   I SAW IT! I HELD IT! I WATCHED IT COME OUT OF YOU, ALL BLOOD . . . !

**Girl**   No. Please; no.

**Woman** (*to* **Girl**)   You have no baby.

**Girl** (*flat*)   No.

**Man** (*to* **Woman**)   What a wise girl

**Woman**   What a brave girl.

**Boy** (*crying now*)   I . . . saw . . . it; I . . . I held it.

*Response tempi easy now; all gentle except* **Boy**.

**Woman**   No.

**Man**   No.

**Girl**   No.

**Boy** (*sobbing*)   Yes.

**Woman**   No.

**Man**   No.

**Girl**   No.

**Boy**   Yes.

**Woman**   No.

**Man**   No.

**Girl**   No.

**Boy**   No?

**Woman**   No.

**Man**   No.

**Girl**   No.

**Boy** (*pause*)   No.

**Man** (*sighs*)   Well then; we're done.

**Woman**   Yes.

**Man** *and* **Woman** *begin moving upstage;* **Man** *pauses; mild puzzled look;* **Boy** *and* **Girl** *in silent tears – if possible.*

**Man**   Tears! (*Out.*) Tears! (*To* **Woman**.) Tears!

**Woman** (*gentle smile*)   Yes: tears.

**Man** (*to* **Boy** *and* **Girl**, *who are too interior to respond*)   Oh what a wangled teb we weave. Wounds, children, wounds. Learn from it. Without wounds, what are you? If you don't have a broken heart . . . (*Shrugs.*) We'll leave you, then. Don't get up. (*Taking* **Woman**'*s hand.*) Shall we?

**Woman**   *Shall* we?

*They exit; silence;* **Boy** *and* **Girl** *still.*

**Boy** (*still in tears*)   No baby?

**Girl** (*still in tears*)   No.

**Boy** (*more a wish than anything*)   I hear it crying!

**Girl** (*please*)   No; no, you don't.

**Boy** (*defeat*)   No baby.

**Girl** (*begging*)   No. Maybe later? When we're older . . . when we can take . . . terrible things happening? Not now.

**Boy** (*pause*)   I hear it crying.

**Girl** (*pause; same tone as* **Boy**)   I hear it too. I hear it crying too.

*Lights fade.*

*Curtain.*

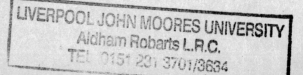